CHORES

P O E M S

Maggie Burton

BREAKWATER
P.O. Box 2188, St. John's, NL, Canada, A1C 6E6
WWW.BREAKWATERBOOKS.COM

ISBN 978-1-55081-963-2
FRONT COVER Saturday's Child © Luanne Dominix

A CIP catalogue record for this book is available from Library and Archives Canada.

We acknowledge the support of the Canada Council for the Arts. We acknowledge the financial support of the Government of Canada through the Department of Heritage and the Government of Newfoundland and Labrador through the Department of Tourism, Culture, Arts and Recreation for our publishing activities.

PRINTED AND BOUND IN CANADA.

Canada Council for the Arts Conseil des Arts du Canada Canada Newfoundland Labrador

Breakwater Books is committed to choosing papers and materials for our books that help to protect our environment. To this end, this book is printed on a recycled paper that is certified by the Forest Stewardship Council®.

Second Printing

For Jack, Ursula, Edith, and Ada

I

II

I

The Midwife

She caught babies in winter,
laid fish to dry in summer,

was eager to sop blood, guts
of anything pierced that needed

her. When the first baby came,
she fished him into her arms,

wiping his face with her thumb,
so enraptured by the sudden touch

of blood that she didn't see
the twin who slithered out

as if on pelvic fin, hidden
by afterbirth, cradled in placenta

into the Old Port salt beef bucket,
destined for the greedy harbour

to be released, returning
to something wet, smelling of home.

The bucket started howling on the walk
to the water, cold night wind

waking small lungs. The father
looked down. As he rubbed

his baby's eyes, sound broke from him, too
like a blow in the nautical chorus.

Chores

i.

Pop snared rabbit, our early morning
catch. The woods were teeming.

I expected its breath to smell
like hops, whiskers to twitch,
eyes to be red,

but they were just brown,
stale.

ii.

Nan skinned rabbit in the kitchen
sink.
        While she worked I eyed
the walls wondering
about the fingerprints always
appearing out of nowhere,
as if leaking out from inside
the old wood. Soot black, sticky
as molasses, they mocked us.
No matter what she tried,
they would never come off.

Her fingers dug in hard,
long rabbit legs splayed
open, skin peeling off muscle.

I watched its body flutter
toward the sink's cold edge,
bouncing off the sides,
blood settling in under Nan's
nails. I chucked the leftovers
to the crows.
                                What else was there to do?

iii.

Nan cooked stew and a fresh
batch of homebrew to tide

us over for the month. Enough
steam rising up the stucco walls

to soak the nicotine stains clean off.
Dark streaks dripping

on baseboard lips, into the humming
mouth of the heater.

iv.

Nan shaped doughboys by hand,
knew just when to let go, rolling
them into the boil.
                                        As down
in the pot went the last, she split
these treats with her chosen.

I watched a pregnant carpenter
take her time, lopsided,
crawling under the table.
As our virgin eyes peeked out
from behind skirts, I laid her
on my plate, waiting
for the jam to harden.
                                                Digging
a grave in the leftovers, inside
a jam and doughboy garden.

v.

Nan hid her fermenting
beer in a rain barrel

behind shrouded closet doors.
It stank up the pink bathroom.

I dared my friends to peek,
to taste the drink I knew

was soft and sweet and meant
to complement the rabbit.

vi.

We set the table and Nan set the stage
for dinner. I played cowboys
in the bathroom while Pop watched
The Man Who Shot Liberty Valance.

John Wayne at the bar
asking, "Well, now; I wonder what
scared 'em off?"
I mouthed along, like church

time. "You know what scared 'em—
the spectacle of law and order
here, risin' up out of the gravy
and the mashed potatoes."

vii.

I capped beers with Pop.
He stood tall, a smoke
dangling from his lips,
face and eyes into measuring
sugar, the sound of the capper
gave me the willies.

Golden booze trickled
from my hose into the mouths
of empty repurposed bottles,
the space behind their labels
still sticky where we ripped them
off. Pop reached for a cap,

        I backed away slowly,
        one eye on the hand

        reaching for his pockets.
        This is the West, sir! I whispered.

Credits rolled. The shadow
of the capper in my hand
on the TV screen.
A shotgun,

                loaded.

Radio Bingo

I sprawl on Nan's bed, paint
my nails red, listen to VOWR's
Hymns for the Quiet Hour, the greatest

opera of our time, a weekly
tragedia lirica where no one gets out
alive. I am the wardrobe supervisor.

The star I dress in slack-pants, blouse,
pastel cardigan, compression socks,
perm, knitted slippers, a billowy,

high-waisted dress. I put on her rings,
squish the spider veins attempting to nest
in soft skin. She changes the station

to the Voice of the Common Man
as the top of the hour news,
the overture, begins. Nan straightens

her wig, enters stage left.
Don Giovanni hides in the living
room corner, double-timing

whiskey and homebrew while Donna
Elvira flies around the stage:
"who will ever tell me where

that scoundrel is? *Ah! Chi mi dice mai*,
I will rip his heart out." She takes
her seat at the kitchen table, stabs

the free spaces with her dabber.
Heavy with gossip, full of fresh smoke
from Player's tub rollies, the air

is thick fresh bread. I hold my breath
as the first number is called.
Behind the radio's tinny mouth,

the announcer is dressed
as Pagliaccio but no one can see
his beautiful face. The sad thought

of him crying into his double-double
kills me. Backstage, Nan does
her warmups, scolds my lazy lack

of makeup, pinching my baby fat,
again. I can bear it no more.
I rise as Norma, proclaim "blood,

blood! Revenge!" on all my relatives.
I chase her from the room,
my fingers down my throat.

The curtains draw. Lace hiding
nothing. Anyone could see us here,
struggling. Dido this time,

Nan laments, "remember me, but ah!
forget my fate," orders another smoke
be set ablaze, a pyre. I click the lighter.

B	I	N	G	O
Nan was	winning	at bingo.	Girls’	night out
we’ve	been here	for days	trying	to win.
The fog	of the	FREE	smoking	side
of the hall	so thick	we swim	in it—	swans
floating	above	a collective	common	sense.

B	I	N	G	O
Nan was	preparing	to jump	clear out	the water
if	she won.	On the	hitch	for B12
she'd fly	through	FREE	night skies	with an
envelope of	loose	twenties—	cash	to buy
enough	B12	to get	through	the winter.

B	I	N	G	O
Maybe	she'd	be happy	enough	she'd want
to live	forever	if she	was rich—	her smoking
an obvious	issue—	FREE	quitting	of her own
volition.	I imagine	her lungs	growing	back
made	of steel	regenerating	like a baby	starfish.

B	I	N	G	O
Maybe	gambling	wastes	my time.	I crawled
instead	around	the floor	of the hall	foraging
for change	scooping	FREE	pennies	dimes
stuffing	them in my	khaki	green fanny	pack—the
apocalyptic	fashion	statement	Y2K will be	remembered for.

B	I	N	G	O
Maybe she	would put	a curse on	the miser	calling B9.
Arseholes	wants me	to have	nothing!	Neither
trace at all	of the grace	FREE	o' God	here today!
Nan yelled	slamming	her fists	slamming	her tinnitus
her ill wishes	ringing	for hours	inside her	ears.

B	I	N	G	O
If she	won	she would	buy me	a few
more	pull-	tabs—	the dissimilar	lines
of rejected	luck	FREE	already	sprawling
under	the bingo	tables	like	the kind
that litter	the ground	during	summer	festivals.

B	I	N	G	O
If she	won	we kids	would	have fun
playing	with others’	ripped-up	bingo	cards
under	the tables	FREE	fashioning	spectacular
boats	we could	paddle	around	though
no one	taught us	how	to row—	we’re girls.

B	I	N	G	O
If she	lost,	us	grand-	daughters
of angry	ladies	who	just	wanted
a bit	of pocket	FREE	money	that
didn't	come	from	the husband's	sock
drawer	would be	driven	home	quiet.

B	I	N	G	O
If I won	I'd hide	my	money	under
my	pillow	when	I got	home
knowing	all my	FREE	winnings	would just
disappear	in the	fog.	If I	kept
her	from all	this cash,	would she	quit?

B	I	N	G	O
Well	Nan?	No luck	she says	I notice
the ladies	around me	half-	praying	half-
dead, I	imagine them	FREE	painting	war
lines	under	their eyes	with daubers	casting
a spell—	dark	magic	to win	at bingo.

B	I	N	G	O
We	glared	at that	benevolent	man
behind	the bingo	balls	picking	his
lips—	the dead	FREE	skin and	dandruff
flaking	falling	into	his	glass of
Pepsi	the ice	long	since	melted.

B	I	N	G	O
The bastard	is prepared	to call	out	for hours
yet	until	the jackpot	goes,	his
skin	will keep	FREE	shedding	like
the snake	he is.	Someone	will win	at bingo
someone	will get	money	for	smokes.

Smoke Made Mares' Tails

Mares' tails and mackerel scales
make lofty ships to carry low sails
—old rhyme

i. Mares' tails

For me, mares' tails were smoke forming
over the tea table after Nan let me help.

She lit a smoke, I felt the lighter click
inside my lungs. It was home.

I considered taking it up, but was nervous,
didn't know how much lung was left

in my scrawny body. Nan's were at ten
percent. Sometimes Nan doubted her

smoke, she peered through streams of gossip,
told me I reminded her of women she knew,

but couldn't remember exactly who,
their faces carried away by time's lofty ships.

ii. Mackerel scales

The old sun-bleached siding on the house,
a mackerel sky, still-stained curtains wet on the line,

rain helped the mackerel scales in the compost heap
find their final resting state in stinking earth,

become roses. The storm came out of nowhere.
The curtains on the line were washed a second time.

The sky birthed a woman so thorough, so good
at chores that the rose bushes

would have no leaf left unscrubbed, even after
Nan leaves me behind.

When her pounding fists of rain
let me be, her sunny side came out,

saying I'll wash, duckie, you dry.

I Rolled Smokes

Gardening is work too, li'l chicken,
doesn't mean I am unemployable.
I just prefer this to minimum wage.

Do you think a bush should go here?
We could get one still burning.
You could plant it on my garden grave.

I could lie here, secure, after my lips
eat up the thin paper. Feel your death
wish weight one last time.

Remember the white tub of baccy
the chick-chick of the roller.
Five cents a smoke I used to give you.

You helped, babe. Lungs only last so long,
anyway. Don't worry about it. I'd rather
really live while I'm alive, you know.

Clay Pipes

I wanted to be an archaeologist.
The holes in my backyard were dug by me.

I roped off sections
of my mother's flower beds, destroyed
daffodil bulbs, cut worms in half,

displaced migratory snails, catalogued
every little piece of clay, bone, plates. I wanted
to know whose it was. My father

explained there was a forge here. As if fire
could account for all of this. I glued a pipe
back together, MADE IN NEW GLAS—

appeared almost whole. I brought it to my lips
and my lungs tried on an ashy coat
like my ancestors'. Fishing men, or kneeling

women, bent backs over potato beds
over mounds of capelin
digging in for winter.

Hands That Knew Heat

As granddaughters we knew without prompting
the fun of exploring ancestral breeding grounds,

draping tiny wrists with ionized bracelets, tracing
the faces of fat terracotta fertility pendants

that were just Red Rose hedgehogs. Lifting trinkets
from her brassy chest of costume jewellery,

clipping on earrings, her rosaries around our necks
as pearls. We read the sock drawer family history,

antediluvian newspaper clippings confirming
what happened. Jelly on night tables next to bibles

collecting dust. These bedrooms, a shrine to
ambivalence, though sometimes we drew hearts

in dust settling down or squeeze out some goo,
have it crack in hands that knew heat only in creation.

Knock Knock

I cheated at Crazy Eights
while Nan went to make me some toast.
A hand like a foot I got,
I complained as she scraped burnt bits
rhythmically into the sink.
While she was bent over the Imperial margarine,
I snuck the two of spades into my fan

to make her pick four.
I would say, giggling,

—Knock, knock
last card.

Foiling my plans flat like highlights,
Nan changed the suit to clubs.
Hands cupped around everything
I held dear, I was out of luck.
'Spose we'll dart to the shop
the once, she said carelessly, then,

—Knock, knock
last card.

Last Card

I felt the sinking, childlike guilt of cheating
while Pop came in to roll smokes,
tapping his nails fast in a three-two-one

pattern onto the counter, looking right
through me, while he was talking in Morse code
to the Lone Ranger.

Knock, knock—
last card.

I snuck the two of spades back into the deck,
wouldn't want to risk being Wanted,
and have cowboys come

'round, looking for trouble.
I placed a red eight on the table, putting out
my hand as fast as possible, as yet unable

to handle being saddled with silent
knaves, kings and queens holding court.
Some hand, I said,

Knock, knock—
last card.

Old Souls

After swimming at the beach
we had sand stuck to our *labia majoras*.

Still not old enough
to have gotten a shower before,

heat coming from one fixed source
too much for the adults to agree to,

there was not much we could do
about the sand unfortunately

as bath water just rearranged the dirt
on the frontispieces of our selves.

We wondered,
what would it be like

as a grain of sand
free to move around
the world anytime
you wanted to go

to be free to harden or change into glass
in a furnace at a thousand degrees?

Hum

We cleaned out our belly buttons
with a sable hair paintbrush
I brushed away her lint
she brushed away mine—
we could never sleep, lying
still on the top bunk, listening—

the hum of the fridge

the hum of the dehumidifier

the hum of her mother's deep
throaty hum singing hum to him

the hum of animals in the wild

the hum of the high notes

the hum of the wind
passing through her zenith.

Mustnttouch

We were so much alike we could show
each other our foreign parts and finally see
ourselves. We'd always known better
than to look, definitely better than to touch.

Until now: quickly daring each other
after school, we stood at opposite
ends of the room. From there we

could finally see the body part that
we heard the adults call

Mustnttouch. Duck.

We looked for yellow beaks. Orange toes.
Brown feathers. Nothing was there.

We were so much alike
we could finally give each other
courage to feel the glint of the hand
mirror's reflection on the insides
of our thighs, taking comfort in this new

knowledge that the sun won't actually burn
you in the time it takes to look at your own

body. In fact, the sun will highlight
the colours you see. You will at once
understand the rest of your insides
are also beautiful.

You'll feel heat,
wonder where is it coming from?
Red heart. Blue veins. Everything is there.
Just touch.

Burning the Anthills

I survey mounds of raised earth,
turn over rocks marking danger zones,
check on the progress of secret tunnels,
wonder just how deep they go.

Sandy hills poked with sticks, the initial
provocation an annual tradition
before the gas-pouring ceremony begins.
I strike a match for black beasts below.

I can almost hear their little feet—
thip thip thip—sounds like fingers
flicking whimsy off a girl's forehead.
I watch their babies, swaddled,

evacuated in goopy white blankets,
dream-nursing their way through ascension.
I want these children of ant queens, perfect
copies of perfect woman-made women,

produced outside of birthing, mothers whole
and healthy, seeking pleasure. I drop the match.
Panicking, they crawl up my thighs, hoping
to fall asleep somewhere warm and familiar.

Transformation Gag

Rake a field confettied with 50/50 tickets,
admission bracelets, barf. Scoop everything
into big black bags. Pop cans will never be
bicycles here—no chance of the transformation
gag the tourists and townies call recycling.
But the beer tent folds in on itself, packs away
its principles like a fitted sheet. The porta-potties
get out of line, trickle their wares into a stream
that meets the sea. Charlie's Moose Burgers
moans as a band of men tear into its long legs,
buckle them into the back of a pickup truck,
break down the concession for another festival.
Hiscock's Wedges Wagon throws a tantrum,
spits squished fries, dressing, gravy on the grass,
bawling like a youngster refusing to leave.
Going home from my summer job, I walk my bike,
too scared to sit. My sweater around my hips,
I sneak a finger down my thigh to check the blood
from the period I just found in the porta-potty.
The chance the soggy white patch I scrape off
my shoe was once a potato? Roughly 50/50.
This transformation will soon be complete.

II

Bad Date

i.

My tub finally clean, I climbed into murky water,
sluicing armpits in yellowed watercolours

of Hurricane Matthew, his October visit a warning:
don't dare soak a body so soon after weathering

a storm. I was ready for real grass to grow
out of the drain, between the streaming sighs

of water, the pump waking up finally
to sediment, to seeds germinating in rust, coughing

up a lung all morning long. Copper claws, tub feet
now a cow's tasty heel, the drain

my mouth, sipping foot soup. My garlic grew
too tall, little green tips poking out, like the excited

penis of a shaggy tan terrier. Potatoes sprouted
extra limbs, onions pickled themselves, at ease

with the way they smelled. I filled the slow cooker
with these old ingredients, cursing the flavourless

toppings on such a fresh cut. The tummy-turning
anticipation of dinner having itself ready on time

was too much for me to bear, so I made breakfast:
avocado toast, decorated with chia seeds,

tiny flecks of obsidian on emerald jewels. Things
I knew my date would never consent to eating.

ii.

My couch cushions bore water
once, old stains spreading down

from where I laid my hair, wet
after I walked back from downtown in the rain.

My toes found the underside
of the couch's body.

I rubbed them along erratic teeth, staples someone
lovingly tapped in, one layer over another,

only to catch in the frayed, translucent apron,
ripping spaces between old wood slats. I considered

sealing them up again. Spent shards of material fall
soundlessly, as if a kitten was somehow involved.

I forgot to close the curtains. In my room
I got into a revealing piece

of myself. Hair swooping back
over my forehead like wings, I closed the closet

door and waited for him to call.
My closet, a private place, mine, lost in time.

My toes soon found the corners of my bed

without any blankets to suffocate them.

Focusing on the friction of my head
on board helped me maintain a steady pulse.

Counting to ten, over and over, working
on delivering an optimal performance.

Mentally practicing violin, visualizing
the struggle to disguise the staleness

of the tinny open E-string. Imitating Heifetz,
trying to match his vibrato to the current mood,

failing. Hands controlling nothing, except
the space between us. Even though

I told him I hate it when things touch my face.
And then though I watched me, I was not me.

I was Pratt's Donna, sock lines permanently
etched into my legs. I was orphan

Sara Crewe, wailing in the circle of my own
imagining in the attic, cursing magic

for letting a bad thing in. I was Laura Palmer
in a smooth velvet room for twenty-five

years listening to men talking, listening

to perfect jazz, about to finally kiss Agent Cooper

if only I could just stop being dead
for a second. I was Susie Salmon, like the fish,

about to make love to a ghost. I was magic.
I lost my head, too, watched it roll

under my bed. From there I could see myself,
see every bad date walk in the door. I rolled my eyes

at the spectacle of life. Once even I
was delicate. Our supper, uneaten, cold,

on the counter. I opened a new can of peanuts,
the can my mouth peeled open as if

I could laugh at any time.

iii.

Scrubbing mould
off the bottom edge of my bathtub,
where caulking meets tile
meets the tub's body,
sweat pooling between
creases of neck fat,
my hands slipped on wet floor, chin
hitting top lip of the tub. As I lay still
on the floor, bitten tongue lolling
forward to wash the front
of just-brushed teeth in blood,
I saw last night's date there with me
all over again. A tuft: grey, oval,
light and fluffy, down gracing
a gosling's head, a part of him,
his belly button, of me, undressing
him. I watched for a while until

someone
not me
blew it
away.

Cleaning Out the Freezer

In and out like a lion I hunt by morning
moon and freezer light, like what was seen
by men through fog on frozen floes.
You know sealers hunted in the Narrows?

I scoop out forgotten chicken thighs in shame,
pick blueberries off frost, look for wild
strawberries lost in margarine tubs. My hands,
Spring breaking ice apart, bread in cold soup.

The long and hungry month of March is here.
It's all the same today, really, the price of cigarettes
being what it is. Learning how to live
alone, I appreciate the constants.

Like those who came before me,
I relish frugality, delight in the necessity
of self-preservation, freeze box-mix
pancakes for later, half-eaten by picky mouths,

syrup-wet backs, soaked so thoroughly
they never thaw. My pancakes died deep
in the freezer, stuck in the ice for months
before anyone noticed, next to the thyme.

Cleaning Out the Fridge

Shelves weighed down with unnecessary bits
of lives sustained by convenience—
store turkey, dressing & gravy
sandwiches. Packets of tartar sauce resting
in vegetable drawers drowning in old
cucumber juice. *You are saucy enough*, I hear Nan say,
fishing them out. Ancient jars of pickled wieners
from a time when my ex was
trying new things and I told him
I would soon say *I told you so*.
My mouth puckers into a shape I remember
from when flippers were cooked, the grossness
of this Saturday chore too much for me,
the jar whips out of my hand, breaks everything.
I don't sweep it up. Glass will probably settle
in my feet in pieces too small to feel anyway.

Cleaning Out the Fish Tank

The fish lived for a while
on bits of bloodworm from a container,
bubbling happy thoughts to the surface
for a few days whenever I cleaned
his home. I wanted to see the evaporation
lines marking time down the sides. I guess
I wanted to see how quickly organic matter
could decompose in water. Little black

flakes of fish looking like food resting
on rainbow rocks at the bottom.
I was jealous, I wanted to see
what mattered. Can't make this house
feel like a home no matter what I do.
I made this bed. I will lie in it.

Checking the Mousetraps

I wait by the hole in the wall.
There have been scratchings.
A child again, I'm excited
to meet my new friends.

Grow up, the voice in my head
tries to remind us: we are here
to trap, dispose.
I set out tiny slices of cheese

on sweet little paper plates,
get forks and knives ready
on dollhouse tables.
I look through old toy boxes,

a furniture bank of dreams
look for helpful things
I could donate to the cause.
Mother mouse could use a stroller.

Tweezing my Nipplebrows

There. I've done it.
I've invented a new chore for women
to add to a pencil case of pointed
remarks, to write in notebooks
with the date stamped neat
on the inside cheek. You should thank me.
I am your worst fear, personalized
and personified, my fingers are short and fat,
just like yours.
I count five hairs
(last week there were only two).
The tweezers open up, beak wide, and bite.

Changing the Sheets

I can't put the cover on alone.
My body, an apple in a warm mouth,
I dissolve until I am Eve, Snow White,
William Tell, my grandmothers,

until
I am falling deeper into racing
thoughts
            icannotsleep   falling
into a pit of   chickens, geese

pecking ceaselessly
I get up
give up.

Hooking a Rug

The therapist said don't
spend so much time in bed!

Sitting on my bed-
room floor I hook a clothesline scene
until my hand-dyed rags are
laundry, washed, drying
in flaps by the ocean,

each wave of colour
bright as the backs of beetles,
blue as the twinkling eyes of babies, bears.

I hook a robin. In her mouth
a deconstructed nest—
twigs, leaves, grass, sprigs
of lavender, escaping the tree
alone in one piece in the dark
of night.

Packing for Mars

For Justin Dawson

Curiosity was born here. I watch from home
as NASA sends postcards from a planet
ruled by robots. They spend their weekends
creating quiet hierarchies as they play
in the sandbox, explore the South Pole,
waddle around like emperor penguins.

Ever since Viking landed on our dusty neighbour
last century, our assumptions of unsophisticated
microbial life remain unchecked, while really, robots
are busy taking coats for patrons of the robot symphony.

The composition of Mars is Holst on repeat.
Broadcasts come to Earth as fast radio bursts.
We mistake the low staccato of Mars' string section
for failed alien communication.

I scroll through the photos in bed, whistling happy
birthday to myself, homesick for Mars as my island home
storms and the seas rise around me.

Emptying the Vacuum

The fullness of the bag surprised me,
contents spilling out like a day
on the beach, time wasted.

I did it. I disturbed rows of dust
bunnies lying on character-print
beach towels, eating chips
left out from last night's party, gone
soggy from damp sand.

I scattered clods of incidental
tobacco, gifts once given to carpet
while secret lovers passed notes
under picnic tables.

I toppled towers of ash, grieving
for their shapes, their falls from grace,
from great heights silent,
as they change back to carbon.

How could I have emptied it,
knowing what I know?

Cleaning Out the Sock Drawer

Always knew I wouldn't match
socks, but I thought I'd at least
have the discipline to bleach them,
lay them out to sort, to place the unmatched
in neat rows in a lined drawer.

Thought I would sew
scent into flowery satchels,
would care to protect my underwear
from staining, whiten my socks,
my teeth, pluck unruly eyebrows.

Turns out panty-liners, eyebrow-liners,
drawer-liners are luxury items
I cannot afford to think about.

Turns out I can't
stomach the smell of bleach.

Watering the African Violets

I can make my own sugar, honey;
I'm no shrinking violet. I dance
in my crown, though once in purple rage

I rotted as you dripped reckless water
on my head. I am just not into pretending
winter is not the worst. Helpless for now

I watch you deadhead my middle
for the first time since I gave you
these brightest blooms.

Now we wait. Let the petals fall as they will.

Why is it easier to write
about hard things like fault
lines cleaving than how it feels to be

a beautiful woman at the plant store
lifting violets from cart to trunk
as her skirt hem shatters shadows

on the afternoon sidewalk,
tiny catapults throwing light
as if it were infinite in supply.

Doing the Dishes

I put my hand in deep.
Dishwater a familiar warmth in this house,
alone. I feel now for the curvy
edge of the dinner plate, my nails pick
off the hardened pecks of flour,
rubbing patches on the small of the plate's back
to elicit a response.

Capelin clinging to unseasoned cast iron,
the pan's weight in my hands increasing
by the second with tail parts, fin parts
soaking in boiling water, bits of bodies
left on dinner plates thwarting my efforts
to kill any last traces of life until, heaving
with effort, I fish some side vegetables
from the bottom of the sink, placing
shrunken peas on the counter
a trail of crumbs to help me find my way
back to the beaten path, as the *Evening Newshour*
sounds the sundown-in-winter alarm.

Wiping Down the Counters

Exasperated from the cleanup,
from so much endless scrubbing,
I rest here on the kitchen floor awhile,
still listening as NTV's Jim Furlong gives me

Today in History, reminds me
of that global context, his smooth
voice so nice in troubled times, Jim, telling

me of a stirring, deep inside
I thought was dead, Jim, still
talking, reminding me of a winter
where the snow was in banks so caked
with creamy ice they stayed until summer
and the old harbour was chock solid with seals

and harpoons and I now believe
with all my heart the stirring is true and suddenly

I feel my body
become a breakwater—

    I rest there,
    looking down at my stomach, still going strong

breathing in the draft from the cupboards
under the damned kitchen sink. I told my family
I'd fix it or call somebody who could do the job.
I rest there, looking at my pruned fingers, tracing
the lines on the linoleum, up and down

until I come

to my senses
and finish

wiping down
the counters.

I Watch You, Beheading

I hear them, singing, rehearsing,
lamenting, performing an ode to the freedom
of oceans somehow still resonating, settling
in my ears for me to live with.

The tendons on the backs of your thumbs
startle me as you pop off their heads.
I am struck by the quick parallel lines that appear
only to recede again under thin skin of hands.
Did you catch my eyes?

> I see myself joining the nautical chorus,
> all of us warbling together as my head
> plops on top of their never-closing mouths,
> voiceless vertebrates in the kitchen sink.

I panic. Imagine you, pulling up
the base of my skeletal self, fingers
tugging at it like a piece of knitting
needled so tight it would never fit anyway.

Peeling Pomegranates

She slices a pomegranate down the middle,
the juice spreads, blood across her palm.
I've always tried to scoop out the seeds
one by one, but she knows better.

Its inverted pale flesh
honeycombs dripping
baby bees into her deep bowl.
I put my heart on my sleeve and tell her
everything I know:

before they develop pigment
in soothsaying eyes, larvae wriggle
in a dish of liquid food
prepared by nurse bees. It is milky,

not quite opaque. We have seen it before
on our fingers. Future queens feast
on royal jelly, dietary supplements, fertility
stimulants and vitamin B. Bee heads and legs

differentiate as they transform into
pupae. Skin shrivels, hair sprouts
like the regrowth of hair after I first shaved

down there. Finally, I can say the name.
Mons pubis. Fingers rubbing rubies,
I buzz to her open hands.

Robin Soup

i.

Remember bone soup from the dead
of winter, its ambiguous origins—
what was roasting in her oven?

Nourish your imagination. Love
your delicate malleus, incus,
stapes, let them ring with tales

of disobedience. *Check on the bones*,
her voice echoes. You are Gretel
walking toward the open oven door.

Set the trap on the clothesline
post, sprinkle it with bread crumbs,
try not to get any on the fresh-

washed tablecloth. Fall at least once,
sprain a wrist, twist an ankle, what's the diff?
Bone is bone. Let go.

ii.

Jump out of your hiding tree
as the robin falls for bread, trap
body and all drop to sodden ground.
Silently scurry together in last
year's grass. The blood-red-breasted
bird is less like a fowl,
more like a flying ace field mouse
shot down over the open sea
quietly whistling a native song
on enemy land to find some comrades
but getting found instead.

iii.

Comb robin out into trembling
hands. Imagine eating it whole.
Hide your head in shame behind

the flapping wings of the tablecloth.
Imagine the buoyancy of bird bones
in broth, tiny pockets of air letting

marrow escape. Now you can hear
the coming silence of a full belly.
Taste the robin, accented by salt pork,

her homemade bread heavy, soapy
in your mouth. Follow those crumbs
to a candy house. Gulp down

the last drop of soup. Look at yourself
in the bottom of the bowl. Look
at yourself in the bottom of the bowl.

ACKNOWLEDGEMENTS

First off, thank you to my family for your never-ending support and encouragement over the years. Finding the time for poetry when young children are involved is not an easy thing to do. This book could not have been written without the support of my ex-husband Chris McGee and my current partner Michael Collins, who shared the work of parenting with me as I wrote.

Thank you to Arts NL and the City of St. John's for providing grants that supported my writing time. And to *Riddle Fence* for being the first to publish me. Thank you to the various journals in which these works first appeared: *Grain*, the *Malahat Review*, *Newfoundland Quarterly Online*, *Prism*, *Riddle Fence*, *Room*, and *Voices of Eve*.

Many people helped shape the poems in this collection, especially my editor George Murray, and Nicole Haldoupis, Claire Wilkshire, and Rhonda Molloy at Breakwater. To my writing group, Anna Swanson, Matthew Hollett, Tia McLennan, and Don McKay, thanks for making sure my tenses agree with one another. Thank you to all my generous friends who took the time to read various iterations of this book, especially Giles Ayers, Daniel Cowper, Elisabeth de Mariaffi, and Robin Durnford. To Mary Dalton, I have so loved all of our conversations about Newfoundland and Labrador poetry and culture. Thank you to Megan

Gail Coles for believing in me way back when and making sure I've kept my fire going ever since.

Thank you to my dear friend Luanne Dominix for creating the beautiful art that's on the cover.

NOTES

Of special note, the "Nan" character throughout these poems is intended to be a tribute to and a collage of sorts of a typical Newfoundland matriarch; "Nan" does not refer to any one individual.

In "Chores" the quotations and italicized passages are from John Ford's 1962 western, *The Man Who Shot Liberty Valance*.

"Radio Bingo" references VOWR's *Hymns for the Quiet Hour*. VOWR is a radio station in St. John's, and *Hymns* is one of their programs.

Another radio station, VOCM, is referenced as the "Voice of the Common Man."

The line "[w]ho will ever tell me where that scoundrel is? *Ah! Chi mi dice mai*, I will rip his heart out" is one I have taken some creative licence with from Donna Elvira's aria "Ah, chi mi dice mai," from Mozart's 1787 opera, *Don Giovanni*.

Pagliaccio is the stage name of the character Canio from Leoncavallo's *Pagliacci*.

The priestess Norma is the titular character from Bellini's *tragedia lirica*. In the finale of *Norma*, act 2, scene 3, soldiers chant "War, war!" Norma proclaims "Blood, blood! Revenge!" before being asked to decide who will be sacrificed in order to complete the pre-war rites. When faced with killing her lover (the enemy Pollione) or sacrificing their shared children, Norma asks that a pyre be constructed for her.

Dido and Aeneas is Purcell's opera about Dido, Queen of Carthage. The quotation "remember me, but ah! forget my fate" is from Dido's Lament, "When I Am Laid in Earth." Dido orders a pyre be built to burn the belongings of Aeneas, then proceeds to ascend the pyre and stab herself with the sword she gave him:

> When I am laid, am laid in earth, May my wrongs create
> No trouble, no trouble in thy breast;
> Remember me, remember me, but ah! forget my fate.
> Remember me, but ah! forget my fate.

In "Smoke Made Mares' Tails," the italics are a traditional mariner's warning as a rhyme, written in the way I remember hearing it as a child. A wispy mare's tail of cirrocumulus clouds and a mackerel scale formation of altocumulus clouds often indicate high winds, a warm front, and rain.

In "Knock Knock" and "Last Card," the Lone Ranger is a reference to the TV show of that name from the 1950s. The "three-two-one" pattern is a reference to the horses' hooves depicted in the opening theme of the show, the "William Tell Overture," from Rossini's *William Tell*.

In "Bad Date," Heifetz is a reference to the violinist Jascha Heifetz. Pratt's Donna refers to Mary Pratt's 1987 painting "This Is Donna." Sara Crewe is the name of the main character from Frances Hodgson Burnett's book *A Little Princess*. Laura Palmer and Agent Cooper are characters in David Lynch's series *Twin Peaks*. Susie Salmon is the main character of Alice Sebold's *The Lovely Bones*.

In "Changing the Sheets," William Tell is once again referenced. Snow White is the name of the main character from the nineteenth-century German fairy tale. Eve is a woman from the book of Genesis.

"Packing for Mars" refers to the Viking project, part of NASA's Mars exploration program. Gustav Holst's *The Planets: I. Mars, the Bringer of War* is the "composition of Mars" referenced herein.

In "Doing the Dishes" and "Wiping Down the Counters," the *Evening Newshour* and *Today in History* are NTV programs.

In "Robin Soup," the reference to Gretel comes from the German fairy tale "Hansel and Gretel."

Newfoundland poet MAGGIE BURTON is a multi-genre writer, professional violinist, and municipal politician. Burton holds a Bachelor of Music degree from Memorial University and has spent much of her career teaching with the Suzuki Talent Education Program and playing with the Newfoundland Symphony Orchestra. *Chores* was awarded the 2024 Griffin Canadian First Book Prize, received a silver medal in poetry from the Independent Publisher Book Awards, and was shortlisted for the Gerald Lampert Memorial Award. Burton's poetry explores the social and physical realities surrounding women's domestic labour, sexuality, and relationships through a queer, feminist, working class lens. Burton writes and lives on the Avalon Peninsula, where she is raising her four young children.